FUSSY GUSSIE
AND THE
MAGIC POND

BY KAREN BENEDICT

ILLUSTRATIONS BY STEFANIE GEYER

Fussy Gussie and the Magic Pond

Copyright © 2023 Karen Benedict.

All rights reserved. No part of this book may be reproduced or transmitted in any form or by any means, electronic or mechanical, including photocopying, recording, or by any information storage and retrieval system, without writtenpermission from the author.

Published by Birdhouse Press

Printed in United States

ISBN: 978-1-990480-04-1

Names, characters, and places are products of the author's imagination.
Front cover image, illustrations, and book design by Stefanie Geyer.
To see more from the illustrator visit StefanieGeyerIllustration.com.

10 9 8 7 6 5 4 3 2 1

This Book Belongs To:

_____

Gussie was a little chick with a lot of energy.

She loved jumping in mud puddles and chasing butterflies. Her tail wiggled as she walked. And every now and then, she liked to stick her tongue out.

When it came to adventure, Gussie would try anything as long it wasn't a new food!

One morning, Mama Goose took Gussie to a beautiful grassy meadow.

As she munched on the tops of the grass, she said,

"Gussie, this grass is the freshest in all of the forest. Wouldn't you like just a taste?"

But Gussie was more interested in playing among the delicious flowers and watching the bees buzz from place to place.

The next day, Papa Goose took Gussie to the nearby cornfield. Showing Gussie the plump, golden corn he said,

"Gussie, this is the sweetest corn I have ever tasted. Wouldn't you like just a bite?"

Gussie stuck her tongue out and made a funny face.

"Yuck. Besides, I'm not hungry, Papa. Can I please play with that little bunny for a little while instead?"

So, Gussie spent time playing in the cornfield instead of eating.

That evening, Grandma Goose came to visit.

"**Gussie,**" Mama said. "**Grandma brought you something special!**"

Gussie came running to greet Grandma and to see what she had brought her.

"**Hi, Grandma!**" she said. "**What do you have in your basket? Is it a gift?**"

"**Indeed, Gussie!**" Grandma said, pulling out a bunch of oat sheaves from her basket.

"**The best kind of gift! These are delicious oats!**"

"**Eww! I don't like oats!**" Gussie said, and she walked away.

"I don't know what to do," Mama told Grandma Goose.

"Fall is just around the corner. Soon, we will have to begin our long flight south for the winter. But Gussie is not strong enough to fly that far. And if she doesn't eat up, she never will be!"

Suddenly, Mama Goose had an idea.

That night, as she tucked Gussie in, she told her a bedtime story about a magical pond not too far away from where they lived.

"There are dragonflies and butterflies darting around in the sky, and the songbirds sing the sweetest tunes you've ever heard," Mama said.

"There are painted turtles and frogs and colorful fish swimming in the pond."

Gussie's eyes widened with wonder.

"Can you take me there, Mama?" she asked.

"I could take you," Mama said, **"but . . . no, nevermind. You wouldn't appreciate it."**

"Oh, no, Mama. I will. I promise."

Mama looked at Gussie.

"**The thing is,**" she said, "**the only way to see the magic is to eat the wheatgrass that grows at the pond. But I know you'd much rather play than eat.**"

"**Oh, please, Mama. I want to eat the wheatgrass and see the dragonflies and butterflies,**" said Gussie.

"**Can you please, please, take me there?**"

Mama looked at Gussie for a long time.

Finally, she nodded.

The next morning Mama, Papa, and Gussie Goose went to the magical pond.

As they waded into the warm water, Papa said, **"Gussie, would you like a ride on my back? I can take you to the wheatgrass."**

Gussie excitedly hopped on Papa's back, and together the two swam slowly through the long stalks of wheatgrass.

Papa stopped when he reached the middle to nibble on a few stalks.
"Would you like to take a taste, Gussie?" he asked.

Gussie reluctantly took a nibble.
Then she took a bigger bite.
It was good! Really good!

Gussie looked around and gasped as she saw dragonflies fly from the water.

"What are those, Mama," she asked. "I have never seen anything so beautiful!"

"Those are dragonflies, dear!" said Mama. "Look how colorful they are!"

On a rock, Gussie spied a painted turtle sunning itself. She hopped off Papa's back and swam up to the painted turtle.

"Hello, Turtle. Do you want to play?" Gussie asked.

The turtle lifted his head slowly, looked at Gussie, and then slid underwater.

Gussie dove underwater after him, and the two began to chase each other around the pond.

Something brushed by Gussie's beak and she started giggling. **"Look, Papa, there are fish swimming all around me,"** she said.

In the trees nearby, Gussie heard songbirds chirping **"Listen to that song!"** she said.

"Papa," Gussie said. **"Can I hop onto your back? I want to eat some more wheatgrass. It tastes so good!"**

Papa could hardly believe his ears. Smiling, he said, **"Hop on, Gussie!"**

That night, Gussie could hardly fall asleep.

"Mama, Papa, can we please go back to the pond tomorrow?" she begged. "Please, please, pleaaaase?"

Mama laughed. "Sure, Gussie. If you get some rest tonight, we can go back tomorrow."

The next morning, Gussie rose bright and early, ready to visit the pond.

"Hello, Frog. Hello, Turtle!" she said.

"Hey, Gussie, nice to see you again!" the animals answered.

"Do you want to play catch?" the turtle asked, diving into the water.

Day after day it went this way—Gussie playing and eating as much delicious wheatgrass as her stomach would hold.

And slowly, without her even realizing it, her wings grew stronger and stronger.

Then, one morning Gussie woke up earlier than usual. The air had a chill to it, and she shivered.

"Can we go to the pond again, Mama?" Gussie asked.

But this time, Mama shook her head. **"It's time for us to fly south Gussie! I'll tell you what, why don't we go to the magic pond to say one last goodbye, and we can fly from there?"**

Gussie was sad because she was going to miss all her friends at the magical pond.

But she knew they would be waiting when she got back.

Gussie said her goodbyes, and then, with one last look back, she flapped her now-strong wings and rose into the air.

"Bye, bye, friends and bye, bye, magic pond!" she said. **"I can't wait to see you next spring!"**

The Canada Goose

The Canada Goose, or Branta canadensis, is one of North America's most recognizable waterfowl species. These large birds are known for their distinctive black heads, white cheek patches, and brownish-gray bodies. They have a long, black neck and a broad, flat bill, which they use to graze on grasses and other plants.

Canada Geese form strong pair bonds during the breeding season, and both parents work together to raise their young. They build nests on the ground, using grasses, leaves, and other materials to create a comfortable and secure place for their eggs. The female typically lays between four and eight eggs, which hatch after about 28 days. Goslings are born covered in soft, down feathers and can walk and swim almost immediately.

Canada Geese are migratory birds; some populations travel thousands of miles yearly to breed and feed. They are found throughout North America, from Alaska and Canada to the southern United States and Mexico. Canada Goose is a symbol of North American wildlife and is admired for their beauty, resilience, and adaptability.

www.ingramcontent.com/pod-product-compliance
Lightning Source LLC
Chambersburg PA
CBHW042052050526
44107CB00109B/1115